D1564643

A Crash Course

RideTheUnicycle

RideTheUnicycle.Com

Second Edition

BY GREGG VIVOLO

Ride The Unicycle ~ A Crash Course!
By Gregg Vivolo

Published by:
Gregg J. Vivolo
202 Terrace Avenue
North Haledon NJ 07508-2620
UniPsychler@RideTheUnicycle.Com
www.RideTheUnicycle.Com
Printed by: Instant Publishing
www.instantpublishing.com

ISBN, print edition: 1-59872-316-2

First Printing 2003
Second Printing 2006, revised

Contents

Acknowledgements

This booklet is dedicated in loving memory of my dad, Henry Vivolo, a loving husband to my mom and a dedicated father to my brothers and me. Had dad not opened his bicycle shop back in the early seventies I never would have learned to ride the unicycle. Dad, we love you and miss you!

Thanks to Christine, my loving and dedicated wife and the mother of my four boys. Thanks for not only putting up with me all these years, but for also taking time out of you hectic schedule to help edit and proofread this booklet.

To my brother Glenn, who taught me how to ride the unicycle over 32 years ago. It was Glenn who gave me my first unicycle as a birthday gift about that same time. Glenn also took the time to shoot the pictures for the first version of this book. Thank you on all counts!

A special thanks to my friend, Charles (Chuck) Wildey, for rescuing me from 20 years of misery with my previous employer and also taking the time to shoot the photos for this booklet.

And last but surely not least, I want to thank God. In a day where it's getting increasingly less "politically correct" to acknowledge God, I recognize that I would be nothing without Him. He is my Creator, my Lord and my Redeemer and I thank God, with all my being, for loving me so much that He would lay down His life for me.

"For I am not ashamed of the gospel of Christ: for it is the power of God unto salvation to every one that believeth; to the Jew first, and also to the Greek."

~ Romans 1:16

"Nothing will ever be attempted if all possible objections must first be overcome."

- Samuel Johnson

Chapter One
<u>UNICYCLE HISTORY</u>

The history of the unicycle is somewhat uncertain. The unicycle is thought to have descended from the penny-farthing bicycle of the late 19th century. These bicycles had a large wheel in front, to which the pedals were attached, and a much smaller wheel in the back for balance. Over the years these early bicycles were also called "High Wheelers" or "Bone Shakers". When these bicycles either hit a bump or slowed the rear wheel would come off the ground, forcing the rider to balance on one wheel. Early photographs show unicycles with very large wheels supporting this theory.

Over 100 years later, on June 1st 1982 the International Unicycling Federation was founded in Japan to further the structure and regulation of the sport of unicycling. The Federation sanctioned the first World Unicycling Championship, which took place in Syracuse, New York, in 1984.

"*Every positive change in your life begins with a clear, unequivocal decision that you are going to either do something or stop doing something. Significant change starts when you decide to either get in or get out, either fish or cut bait.*"

- Brian Tracy

Chapter Two
SHOULD I LEARN TO RIDE A UNICYCLE?

While it may be true that anyone can learn to ride a unicycle, it is this author's opinion that not everyone should try. And while learning to ride a unicycle may not be much more difficult than learning to ride a bicycle, it does require a certain level of agility that some may not possess, or may no longer possess due to physical, medical, or other reasons.

In my opinion, those individuals who are prone to accidents or excessively overweight or suffer from heart disease or another medically debilitating disease should re-consider learning to ride the unicycle or at least consult with their physician or primary care provider. I will add to my list those of you who are lawsuit happy. If you're prowling about seeking whom you may devour in your next lawsuit, do the unicycling community a favor and take up the sport of tidily winks instead.

"To climb steep hills requires a slow pace at first."

- Shakespeare

Chapter Three
WHAT IS A GOOD UNI-AGE?

At what age can a child start to learn to ride the unicycle?

I've been asked this question many times and my answer has always been the same. I don't exactly know.

I say this because, while learning to ride the unicycle is a skill which can be learned, balance itself is a part of child development which doesn't occur at the same age for all children. If a particular child has not developed the degree of balance necessary to ride the unicycle, he will not, in most cases, be able to learn to ride the unicycle at this time.

There are always exceptions and occasionally, a child who has not yet developed a sufficient degree of balance will develop it while trying to learn. In actuality, trying to learn to ride the unicycle may help a child develop the skill sooner than they would naturally.

In my experience with teaching children to ride, most children who try to learn prior to having developed a sufficient degree of balance often become discouraged and frustrated and learning to ride is not an enjoyable experience. The child almost always loses the desire to practice and has to be "forced" to practice. In my opinion it is better to wait 3 – 6 months and try again when the child has developed further. If the child is still not ready wait another 3 – 6 months.

With this having been said, there have been times when I have "forced" children to practice because their lack of desire to practice was due to laziness, or a lack of motivation or discouragement and not due to developmental reasons.

In my experience I have found that age 7 - 8 is a good age for most children to try to learn how to ride. At age 7 or 8 most children have developed the degree of balance necessary to learn to ride. At this age they also understand and can appreciate that if they desire to learn to ride it's going to take some time and practice.

"Safety is something that happens between your ears, not something you hold in your hands."

- Jeff Cooper

Chapter Four
UNICYCLE SAFETY

In all my years of teaching unicycling none of my students have suffered any injury greater than a bruised shinbone or minor scrape. This is due to my requiring all my students to take safety seriously and wear the proper safety equipment, including a properly fitting cycling helmet, knee & elbow pads, wrist guards, closed toe shoes (no sandals), a mechanically sound unicycle, and a quiet area void of moving traffic.

During the learning process I also highly recommend the use of rubber pedals instead of metal ones. If the unicycle you're using has metal pedals, go purchase a pair of rubber pedals at your local bike shop. If after my warning you insist on using metal pedals, then invest in a pair of shin guards. You'll be glad you did.

"Being safe is like breathing. You never want to stop."

- Author Unknown

Chapter Five
<u>UNICYCLE ANATOMY</u>

The unicycle is not a very complex piece of equipment and doesn't have many parts; however, some degree of precision must be incorporated in the manufacturing of a unicycle to make it rideable. It's also worth noting that a mechanically deficient unicycle will be harder to learn to ride on than a mechanically sound one.

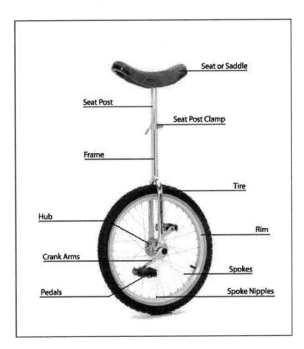

"Nothing can stop the man with the right mental attitude from achieving his goal; nothing on earth can help the man with the wrong mental attitude."

- W.W. Ziege

Chapter Six
<u>UNICYCLING STYLES</u>

Believe it or not, there are several different styles of unicycling. With each style of unicycling come different variations of unicycles. It is not uncommon for a unicycling enthusiast to own several different size and shape unicycles for different types of riding. The entry level style of unicycling for most is recreational riding. Beyond that lie the more advanced styles of riding. Let's take a more in-depth look into the world of advanced unicycling.

Unicycle Racing

Unicycle racing is just that, racing on a unicycle. Categories are usually broken down by wheel size and/or age. Traditionally, riders race a predetermined distance to a finish line where the first one who crosses wins the race. There are, however, other variations of unicycle racing. Unicycle racing is traditionally performed on 20" and 24" wheels. With the gaining popularity of larger wheel sizes it won't be surprising to see racing categories include these larger wheels in the very near future.

Artistic or Freestyle Unicycling

Artistic unicycling includes several different variations of artistic riding. They include competitions for the proficiency of standard and advanced skills. Variations may include music, costumes and choreography while others involve riding in pairs or groups. A 20" unicycle is most common for this style of riding.

Mountain Unicycling (MUNI)

Mountain unicycling, one of the fastest growing styles of unicycling, is much like mountain biking. Mountain unicycles commonly use more durable components, 24" and 26" wheels, and knobby tires for better traction on rough terrain. Though lots of fun, mountain unicycling is more challenging due to the need to navigate around and over the various obstacles associated with dirt trails and mountain terrain.

Trials Unicycling

Trials unicycling is probably one of the most challenging styles of unicycling. It can take place on dirt trails or on a closed obstacle course where riders try to precisely navigate on, over, around and through various natural and/or man-made obstacles. Obstacles may include, but are not limited to, wood pallets, long thin beams, boulder sized rocks, automobiles, steps, pipes, etc...The obstacles in trials riding are only limited by ones imagination and creativity. A very durable 20" unicycle is commonly used for this style of riding.

Touring/Distance Unicycling

With the advent of larger wheel unicycles, such as 28", 29", 36", and the introduction of geared unicycles, touring or distance unicycling is becoming more and more popular. In the same way that touring or riding longer distances appeals to bicyclists, the same holds true for many unicyclists. It is not uncommon to hear of unicyclists riding 20, 30, 50 and even 100 or more miles on their unicycles. As of this writing, touring unicycling is still in its infancy but is beginning to gain some recognition. In 2005 unicyclists were invited to participate in one of the oldest national bicycle race/rides, the Iron Horse Classic, held in Durango/Silverton, Colorado.

Street Unicycling

Street unicycling is one of the more recent developments in unicycling. The aim of the sport is to use natural, urban, and/or specially made obstacles in a given area to make an interesting show. This sport places high demands on the rider as he should master both freestyle unicycling and unicycle trials. But once mastered, this form of unicycling will be more entertaining than other variations because of the great variety of possibilities.

A CRASH COURSE!

Chapter Seven
WHAT SIZE UNICYCLE IS RIGHT FOR ME?

For the beginning unicyclist the correct size unicycle is paramount. It is so important that it could quite possibly make the difference between learning and not learning to ride the unicycle. Fortunately, figuring out the correct size is not rocket science and consists of nothing more than matching the length of the rider's inseam (measured from the rider's crotch to the floor when wearing sneakers) to the correct size unicycle. The chart below illustrates the relationship of inseam length to unicycle wheel size.

INSEAM	UNICYCLE SIZE
22" or Less	16" unicycle
23"	18" unicycle
24" to 29"	20" unicycle
30" or More	24" unicycle

19

For those of you whose inseam is 30" and greater, even though the chart recommends you ride a 24" unicycle, I personally recommend that you learn on a 20" unicycle provided the seat post is long enough so that the unicycle fits you properly. As illustrated in the section on seat adjustment, the rider should have a slight bend in his/her knee when sitting on the unicycle with one pedal at its full extension. If you are over 6 feet tall then you may consider a 24" unicycle but also consider that it may take you longer to learn how to ride.

I recommend a 20" unicycle over the 24" and larger wheels for several reasons. First, the 20" unicycle situates the rider closer to the ground, which lessens the fear of falling. Second, a 20" unicycle is more maneuverable making it easier to turn and control. And third, a 20" unicycle is not as fast as the larger wheel unicycles, which also helps to lessen the fear of falling.

If your inseam is 30" or greater and you desire to learn to ride as quickly as possible, then it is in your best interest to learn on a 20" unicycle.

16" Unicycle   20" Unicycle   24" Unicycle

Once you learn to ride the unicycle you may never need to purchase another one. However, as I mentioned previously, it is not uncommon for a unicycling enthusiast to own several different size and shape unicycles for different types of riding. For example: I still own and ride the 20" unicycle that I learned to ride on over 32 years ago, but it is not the only unicycle I own. Over the years I've bought or built many other unicycles. If you "get into" unicycling, expect to purchase at least one other unicycle some time during your unicycling years.

"*Success is the good fortune that comes from aspiration, desperation, perspiration and inspiration.*"

- Evan Esar

Chapter Eight
<u>SEAT ADJUSTMENT</u>

Proper seat adjustment is important when riding the unicycle, especially while you're learning to ride. Many students of the unicycle try to learn with the seat height much lower than it should be. The thought, albeit incorrect, is to be able to put your feet on the ground while sitting on the unicycle. While this may make one feel more secure, it will more than likely hinder the learning process due to the awkward and cramped position your legs will assume as you try to pedal.

The correct seat adjustment will allow your knee to have a slight bend in it while you sit on the unicycle with one pedal at its fullest extension (see photo). This will facilitate the smoothest pedal rotation and the least amount of stress on your body.

"Those who would attain to any marked degree of excellence in a chosen pursuit must work, and work hard for it, prince or peasant."

- Bayard Taylor

Chapter Nine
WALK BEFORE YOU RIDE

For the beginning unicyclist, by far the greatest challenge to overcome, besides intimidation, is the habit of not leaning forward enough. I would venture to say that because of the fear of falling, the mind's natural defense mechanism is to tell the body to lean back. While, I suppose, it is possible for a student to lean forward too much, in all my years of teaching I have never had a student with that problem.

This concept of leaning forward is so critical; I want you to perform a little exercise that will hopefully help you to understand this important principle. In this exercise I want you to closely examine how you walk. You'll do this by simply taking just one step; but as you take that step I want you to analyze the physiological movement of your body.

Standing straight with your feet together and your arms by your sides, take one step forward. (See photos on next page)

Standing   *Leaning*   *Stepping*

Did you notice your body's very first action in taking that step? Most people would say that the very first action was the movement of the foot forward. But if you do it again, you'll notice that the very first action is the body leaning forward.

Walking, then, is really just our bodies falling forward, with each step preventing us from falling flat on our faces. This same basic action that we've all been doing since 1 or 2 years of age is the same basic action necessary for riding the unicycle. So applying what we've just learned to the unicycle, unicycling is our bodies falling forward, with each pedal stroke preventing us from falling flat on our faces.

Chapter Ten
THE ART OF FALLING

I'm going to go out on a limb here and make you a guarantee. I guarantee that during the learning process you are about to embark upon you **WILL** fall. You will fall very soon and you will fall often. Don't get me wrong; I'm not trying to frighten you, just preparing you for the inevitable.

Falling Backwards - Incorrect

As you know, no matter what you set out to do in life, there is almost always a correct way and an incorrect way of doing things. What you may not know is that falling is no exception. Yes, believe it or not, there is a right way and a wrong way to fall. In the beginning stages of your learning you are going to fall backwards (see photo).

While this is a normal occurrence for every new student, it is the wrong way to fall. You must learn to fall forward. When you fall backward you **WILL** land on your butt, or worse, almost every time. This may increase the risk of injury to your back, elbows and/or head. When

Falling Forwards - Correct

you fall correctly, which is forward, your feet, hands and arms will break your fall more than 99% of the time. It's basic human nature (see photo).

I'm going to make another guarantee here and it is this; if you're NOT falling forward every time it's because you're not leaning forward enough, something I will discuss more in depth in a later chapter.

To alleviate falling, or rather the fear of falling, while learning to ride the unicycle, many have tried using guide ropes, poles, other people or other means to hold themselves up and to help prevent them from falling. If it is your desire to learn the unicycle as quickly as possible, refrain from using these "crutches" as they will only slow the process of learning. I will address this at greater length in chapter Nineteen – "Curb It Or Wall It?"

"Our greatest glory is not in ever falling but in rising every time we fall."

- Confucius

Chapter Eleven
ADDITIONAL NEEDS BEFORE YOU LEARN

In addition to those items recommended in the chapter on safety, you will also need access to a curb approximately 6 - 8 inches high. If you don't have a curb at your disposal, a cinderblock will work or, better yet, a wooden platform made by stacking three or four 2x8 boards approximately 24" in length on top of each other fastened with nails. Just make sure the nails don't stick through the top and bottom boards. Your curb, cinderblock or wood platform will be vital to your learning to ride, as you will soon discover.

The only other thing you'll need is the burning desire to do that which only a relatively small number of people in the whole world can do - ride a unicycle, something that is very cool and loads of fun!

"I am not judged by the number of times I fail, but by the number of times I succeed, and the number of times I succeed is in direct proportion to the number of times I can fail and keep on trying."

- Tom Hopkins

Chapter Twelve
LET'S GET STARTED

Now that all the preliminary stuff is behind us, if you're ready to embark on the process that may change your life forever, then let's get started!

To make the learning process a little easier, I've broken down what I call the "pre-ride" into 6 basic steps. These are: "Curb It!", "The Center Position!", "Sit on It!", "Arms Out!", "Point of Whoa!", and "Ride On!"

Step 1 - CURB IT!

At this point in time, I'd like to introduce you to what will become your best friend for the next couple of weeks. Student meet curb (cinder- block or wooden platform). Curb meet student. Now that the introductions are out of the way, let's move on.

Holding your unicycle in front of you, make sure it's pointed in the right direction. I say this not to insult your intelligence but you'd be amazed how many times I have to tell my students to turn the unicycle around. In case you don't know, the front of the unicycle should face away from you. If you cannot easily determine the front of the unicycle from the rear, look for some of the following obvious and other not so obvious clues: The smaller end of the seat is the front. If a company nameplate or decal is present it is usually on the front. The bolt on the seat post clamp is usually situated towards the rear of the unicycle. And you'll usually find a small "L" for left and/or "R" for right stamped on the inside of each crank arm.

Position the rear of the tire against the curb or platform. (See photo on previous page). If you're right handed, rotate the wheel so that the right pedal is even with the curb (about the 8 o'clock position).

If you're left handed, do the same only with the left pedal (about the 4 o'clock position). Which pedal you decide to set even with the curb is not critical. In my experience, right handed people are more comfortable with the right pedal while lefties are more comfortable with the left.

Step 2 - THE CENTER POSITION

While standing on the curb or platform behind your unicycle, separate your feet approximately the width of the unicycle's pedals.

Now, righties with the right foot and lefties with the left, place the ball of your foot on the pedal even with the curb.

This is the standard learner starting position and I'll be referring to this as the "center position."

The foot, which is now positioned on the pedal, I'll refer to as the "pedal foot" and I'll call the other foot the "resting foot."

Step 3 - SIT ON IT!

As you maintain the "center position" as described in the last section, sit on the seat of the unicycle. Once seated and stabilized, remove your hands from holding the unicycle. The downward pressure on the back pedal or "pedal foot" and your butt in the saddle should keep the unicycle from moving.

Some people may have difficulty sustaining this position for any period of time. That's O.K.! With practice your body's equilibrium will adjust and you'll have no problem.

36

Step 4 - ARMS OUT!

As you maintain the "center position" sitting on the unicycle, raise your arms to about shoulder height with palms down. Whether your arms are locked at the elbows or slightly bent doesn't matter, as they will most likely be flailing about as you try to ride.

Obviously, having your arms out is to help you with side-to-side balance just like a person walking a tightrope holds his arms out or uses a pole.

Resist the temptation to hold the seat while you ride. Holding the seat will hinder your progress and prevent you from learning to balance as quickly as possible. Also resist the temptation to try to catch the unicycle as it falls as this can hinder your progress as well. All your mental energy needs to be focused on balance, not on catching the unicycle.

The only parts of the unicycle that are able to touch the ground and get scuffed are the seat, the pedals and the tire, all of which can be replaced after you learn to ride if you desire. Concentrate completely on learning to ride the unicycle rather than catching it and you will learn to ride much quicker.

Step 5 - THE POINT OF WHOA!

In the section "Walk Before You Ride," we learned the importance of leaning forward. We've reached the point in our lesson where we have to actually do it. To prepare for this next critical step, I'm going to ask you to put the unicycle aside for just a moment to perform another exercise called the standing, leaning, and stepping exercise.

Standing tall with your hands by your sides, lean forward. As you lean and fall forward you'll reach that critical point where your brain tells your body you'd better take a step or else.

I call this the "point of whoa!" Try this exercise a couple of times and remember the "point of whoa!" because it will come in handy real soon.

Now, grab your unicycle and, once again, assume the "center position," sitting in the saddle with your arms out.

Just like in the little exercise we just performed; lean forward slowly and smoothly until you've reached the "Point of Whoa!" (See photo)

Step 6 - RIDE ON!

When you've reached the "point of whoa!," swiftly move your "resting foot" from the curb or platform to the waiting empty pedal and try to ride, remembering to continue leaning forward as you go.

Chances are the first few times you try this, you'll miss the pedal completely. That's OK! In order to hit the pedal, you have to look at it just like a batter hitting a ball. If you don't look at it, you'll never make contact.

Let me share with you what you can expect at this point. If you're like most people, the first few times you try this, the unicycle will lunge forward and you'll fall backward. Again, this is normal at this stage of the learning process. What this means is that while you leaned forward enough to reach the "point of whoa!," you stopped leaning forward once the unicycle started moving. Remember the concept we learned in the section "Walk Before You Ride." Just as walking is your body falling forward with each step preventing you from falling on your face, unicycle riding is your body falling forward with each stroke of the pedals preventing you from falling on your face.

Don't be discouraged. Everything you're experiencing at this point is a natural part of the learning process. Keep practicing.

YOU CAN DO IT!

Now that we've covered all of the six basic steps to riding the unicycle, the next step is simply to practice, practice, practice. As you practice, simply repeat the 6 steps over and over again and progress will come. I guarantee it!

Chapter Thirteen
PRACTICE, PRACTICE, PRACTICE

In all my years of teaching unicycling I've had students who've taken months to learn to ride. I've had others who have learned in a few weeks. And there were those who've learned in as little as a few days. I've even had a few students who learned in just a few hours on a sunny Saturday. Were any of these students any better than another, more agile, or more physically fit? Possibly, but the one indisputable factor that we can attribute to how quickly or how slowly each student learned to ride is the level of desire to learn and the amount of time spent practicing. The student who took a few months to learn wasn't very motivated and might have practiced a few minutes a couple times each week. On the other hand the student who learned in one day was so motivated he wasn't going to bed that night until he learned to ride that unicycle. So how quickly you learn will be in direct proportion to how motivated you are and the amount of time you commit to practice.

"Doing is a quantum leap from imagining... The defense force inside of us wants us to be cautious, to stay away from anything as intense as a new kind of action. Its job is to protect us, and it categorically avoids anything resembling danger. But it's often wrong."

- Barbara Sher

Chapter Fourteen
INCH-STONES COME BEFORE MILESTONES

As you continue to practice, you're likely to get a bit frustrated because in the beginning progress is slow. In fact, progress will be different for each individual. When you begin to get frustrated, grit your teeth and keep going. Before long you're going to reach your first milestone (or should I say inch-stone); you'll ride 6 - 12 inches.

When it happens you'll find new ambition to keep going and do it again or better. Before long, it will happen again. This time you'll go 1 - 2 feet, then 3 feet, now 4, and then 6 - 8 feet and before you know it you'll ride half way across the road. Try to mark your progress with a piece of chalk, as this will automatically raise your bar of achievement.

This slow progress is normal and necessary to tune what I call your built-in gyroscope. Everyone has one; it's what keeps you standing on your feet. The problem is that you've never asked it to work in this capacity before. With each attempt at riding, the gyroscope and the brain are working together to keep your disoriented body upright.

YOU CAN DO IT!

45

The gyro tells the brain that the body is leaning too far this way or that way and the brain is telling the body to compensate by lifting an arm or leaning forward or pedaling harder. In the beginning stages of learning, where the learning curve is the steepest, the difficulty comes because the body can't respond to all the brain's impulses fast enough to keep you on the unicycle. Reactions are slow, clumsy and over-compensation is common. As you continue to practice, your body will adapt and become the finely tuned instrument necessary to not only ride the unicycle, but in time, do tricks and stunts you never dreamed possible.

For a more clinical description of what's going on, let's take a look at how the human brain works. The cerebrum is the thinking part of our brain. It knows what to do, but isn't sure how to do it. The cerebrum, by itself, is terribly uncoordinated when it comes to balance and graceful movement. For natural voluntary actions that require balance and grace, we depend on another part of our brains called the cerebellum. The cerebellum, located at the base of the brain, learns automatically by repetition. Cerebella learning is the key to any skill becoming second nature, including unicycling.

Chapter Fifteen
"TO TURN OR NOT TO TURN"

As you surpass each new milestone it will soon be necessary to turn. What a concept! For some people this won't be a problem because you may already be turning. In fact you may be wondering, "How do I stop turning?" A glimpse at what makes the unicycle turn will not only help you to turn but also help you to correct any unwanted turning.

Generally speaking, the unicycle will only go straight as long as its center axis is 90 degrees or perpendicular to the ground. When the axis is tilted to an angle that is less than 90 degrees the unicycle will turn in that direction. Simply put, if the <u>unicycle</u> is tilted to the right, it will go right and if tilted to the left, it will go left.

To get the unicycle to tilt one way or the other it will be necessary to tilt your hips in the direction you want to turn. If you find it difficult to do this you can try leaning your upper body, from the waist on up, in the <u>opposite</u> direction you wish to turn. The degree to which you tilt your hips will determine how sharply the unicycle will turn. (See photo)

Keep in mind that it doesn't take much of a tilt to get the unicycle to turn. You'll have to experiment with this because it is different for everybody.

Left Turn   *Right Turn*

While one person may require a simple tilt of the head to turn, for another it may take the tilting of the entire upper body. You can practice the hip tilt by performing another simple exercise.

While sitting up straight in a chair (not leaning against the back), shift the weight of your upper body back and forth from one butt cheek to the other. This is the hip tilting action needed to get the unicycle to turn.

In light of this explanation, if you find yourself turning when you don't want to, more likely than not, you're unconsciously leaning more to one side than the other.

To correct this you'll need to check the alignment of your body in relation to the unicycle. While riding, look down at your tire and make sure your head and body are directly above your wheel and not off to one side or the other. You should be able to draw an imaginary straight line from the wheel, up your body, and past your head.

Also check to make sure one arm isn't extended further out than the other. If you can't seem to correct the problem of uncontrolled turning on your own, it may be necessary to have another person watch you to see what is causing your imbalance.

As your built-in gyroscope, your brain, and your body get more acclimated to working together in this capacity, you'll soon be turning on a dime and at will.

Some students may experience a phenomenon where right from the start they plunge headlong into a nasty right or left hand turn with no chance of recovery. Some may actually crank a quick U-turn and ride right into the same curb or platform they started from. The cause of this is almost always related to a poor transition from the "center position" to the "point of whoa!" This transition needs to be a slow and controlled one.

Some students assume the "center position", sitting on the unicycle with their arms out then lunge forward and try to ride. This results in you and the unicycle falling slightly to the side of your "resting foot."

When you start pedaling, you and the unicycle are no longer perpendicular to the ground and a mean uncontrolled turn results.

To combat this, when you assume the "center position," sitting in the saddle with your arms out, make absolutely certain that your unicycle and your body are perpendicular to the ground and your arms are straight out. Lean forward <u>SLOWLY</u> until you reach the "point of whoa!," then transition your "resting foot" from the curb or platform to the waiting front pedal.

YOU CAN DO IT!

"Every positive change in your life begins with a clear, unequivocal decision that you are going to either do something or stop doing something. Significant change starts when you decide to either get in or get out, either fish or cut bait."

- Brian Tracy

Chapter Sixteen
THE PET ROCK: YOUR NEW BEST FRIEND

For most students who don't have the luxury of curbs running up and down both sides of the street you're going to soon become inconvenienced in a big way. You'll reach the point where you can consistently ride 50, 75, 100 feet or more. This is a good thing. The bad thing is that after each ride you have to walk all the way back to your curb or platform to start again. Here's a little trick that I like to use with my students to alleviate the mundane chore of walking back.

 Before we start this exercise find yourself a rock or pebble small enough to comfortably fit into your pocket. You can even hold it in your hand if you prefer. I know this may sound like a strange thing to do at this time but trust me; it will become your new best friend real soon. In fact you can consider it your "pet rock" for a while but don't get too attached because you won't keep it for long.

Continue to practice riding, using the curb or platform, just as you have been up to this point. This time, after a nice long ride, don't bother walking all the way back to your curb or platform to start again. Take your "pet rock" from your pocket and place it on the ground. You're going to use the rock to prevent your wheel from rolling backwards instead of the curb.

Place the wheel of your unicycle against your "pet rock" and assume the "center position," sitting on the seat with your arms out at shoulder height. Place just enough pressure on the "pedal foot" to keep the unicycle against the rock.

In one fluid motion you're going to lean forward and bring your "resting foot" to its waiting, empty pedal and ride. Continue riding in the direction of your curb or platform. Now when you fall off you don't have to walk as far to get back to your curb or platform plus you have the added bonus of doubling your ride time.

If it sounds difficult, it really isn't. Most students will be able to accomplish this with only a few attempts.

I like this exercise because it not only increases your ride time and decreases your walk time but also makes the next step, "Lose The Curb," a whole lot easier to perform.

When you've reached the point where you can actually ride for a while without falling off, your best friends up to now, the curb, platform, and "pet rock," will become a ball and chain, so let's work on getting rid of them altogether. Here's how!

Chapter Seventeen
LOSE THE CURB

The ability to start without the assistance of a curb, platform, or other device is called free-mounting. Free-mounting is an essential skill which we will address at this time.

Once again, assume the "center position" (without the curb, platform or your "pet rock"), sitting on the seat and your arms out at shoulder height.

Place just enough pressure on the "pedal foot" to keep the unicycle from rolling forward, but not too much pressure causing the unicycle to lunge backwards. You should feel the slight pressure of the seat against your crotch as you apply downward pressure on the "pedal foot."

In one fluid motion you're going to slightly increase pressure to the "pedal foot," lean forward, and bring your "resting foot" to its waiting, empty pedal and ride. While this may sound a bit complicated, it's not that bad!

After several attempts, you should be able to perform this quite easily. The key is to look at the empty waiting pedal so you don't miss it. Once you're rid of the curb or platform, you're free to ride anywhere your heart desires. This is true liberation for the beginning unicyclist.

"You are never a loser until you quit trying."

- Mike Ditka

Chapter Eighteen
FUN PRACTICE EXERCISES

When you reach the point where you can ride a good distance, it's time to concentrate on practicing to become proficient at some basic but critical maneuvers.

Since turning is such a critical skill, we're going to concentrate heavily on becoming more proficient at it.

There are three basic exercises that will help move you to the next level of unicycling. These are:

- Circles
- Figure Eights
- Slalom – Cones

These maneuvers are self explanatory but here's a brief explanation of each one to help you get the most out of your practice time.

Circles

Clockwise and counterclockwise circles are just that. The only important thing you want to do is progress from large diameter circles to smaller ones as you feel comfortable doing so. Practice this skill and before long you'll be turning on a dime.

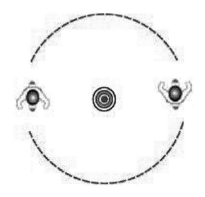

Figure Eight's

The figure eight exercise will prove to help you overcome the challenge of transitioning from a left-hand turn to a right-hand turn and vice versa. Try to ride continuously in a figure eight pattern. Once again you can start with larger diameter circles and progress to smaller diameter circles as you feel comfortable. If you have trouble focusing on making nice figure eights it may help you to place two traffic style cones approximately 10 – 15 feet apart. Try to ride your figure eight around the cones. If you're like most people who don't have traffic cones lying around you can use just about any stationary objects to ride around. Sand pails works real well and can be substituted for cones. As with circles, it's important to reverse your direction from time to time.

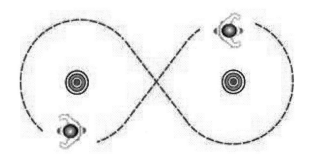

Slalom

Place cones at even distances apart and at a frequency that is easy for you to complete. Start with the cones further apart then move them closer together as you get more proficient at turning. This skill will exercise your ability to plan ahead. You will not be able to complete the slalom without planning the next turn while you are on the current turn.

It is best to practice these exercises in a vacant parking lot or a very quiet street. You should find these exercises challenging but lots of fun. After all, if you've reached this point in the learning process, you're already riding and that in itself is enough to blow your mind. Great Job! Remember to have fun and always wear your safety equipment.

Chapter Nineteen
CURB IT OR WALL IT?

There are many in the unicycling community that feel the "Crash Course" Method also known as the "ride away from the curb" method is an inferior method of learning compared to the "wall" method.

I think learning to ride with the assistance of a wall is a fine idea; however, what I've found over the years is that many beginners don't have easy access to a "good" wall to use while learning. Obviously, a "good" wall is one that has a paved surface adjacent to it.

As I've expressed before, the key to learning to ride the unicycle as quickly as possible is practice. I've also found that if a student has to travel down the street, across town, or wherever to get to that "good" wall, practice is no longer convenient. The student's practice often becomes too infrequent. This hinders his/her ability to learn quickly, which often equates to the student giving up and not learning at all.

This becomes even more of a problem when the student is a youngster who needs his mom or dad to transport him to that place of practice.

I've found that to learn as quickly as possible the student really needs to spend approximately 30 minutes per day practicing. For most students this is only possible when practice is convenient. When the student only needs a curb or platform and his/her unicycle they can almost always go right out their front door and do it. There are no excuses! I believe this is one of the reasons the method I prescribe in this booklet, the "Crash Course" method, has been as successful as it has in getting so many students riding and enjoying this wonderful sport as quickly as possible.

I also like the "Crash Course" method because it helps the student transition to free-mounting much more quickly and easily. When using a wall, the student will learn to ride the unicycle but will not learn to free-mount the unicycle, which the "Crash Course" method does teach.

One of the frustrations I see with most students, even with the "Crash Course" method, comes when they reach a point when they can ride 50 feet or more. Every time they fall off they have to walk back to the curb, platform, or wall to re-mount. This problem is amplified when the student is riding several hundred feet. It is for this reason that I like my students to learn free-mounting as quickly as possible. The "wall" method does not help them in this area. I've seen students who've learned to ride using the "wall" method and never learn to free-mount.

When a student of mine progresses to the point where he or she is riding a good distance, I immediately start the transition to "rock free-mounting." I'll have the student keep a small rock in their pocket. When a student has a good ride of 50 feet or more, I have them turn around, place the rock behind the wheel of their unicycle to keep the unicycle from rolling backwards as they mount it, then "rock" free-mount and ride back towards their curb or platform. The student is able to perform this "rock" free-mount almost immediately.

The ability to "rock free-mount" is an enormous confidence booster. But what I like most about it is that it allows more riding time and less walking time which helps the student learn even quicker.

Once the student is riding well, I'll have them practice normal free-mounting, which, as you can imagine, is picked up almost immediately. The student is then free to ride anywhere his/her heart desires, true liberation for a beginning unicyclist.

I'd like to add that it is not my desire to make an issue out of which method of teaching is better than another. The issue, which is the reason I wrote this book, is all about "spreading the word" about this wonderful sport and to help others learn to ride. If we continue to work diligently, who knows, maybe unicycling will become an Olympic sport some day. Wouldn't that be cool?

All this talk about the "Crash Course" method vs. the "wall" method begs the question; **is there a time when I think it's more appropriate for a student to use the "wall" method over the "Crash Course" method?**

68

Once again, my intention for writing this booklet is not to see how many people I can get to come over to the "Crash Course" camp, but rather, to help as many folks as possible experience and enjoy the wonderful sport of unicycling that I've enjoyed most of my life. So my answer to the question is a resounding "**YES!**"

To some the "Crash Course" method can be a little too intimidating. For these students the fear of falling and getting injured is so great that no matter how hard they try, they just can't muster the courage to continue the learning process. To those people I say, by all means, use the "wall" method. After all, the goal is to learn to ride, which you most certainly can do using the "wall" method.

"Mastery needs practice. Results need efforts. When you understand, success will be yours."

- Puneet Patel

Chapter Twenty
THE "WALL" METHOD (In a Nutshell)

In case you're wondering, the wall method is simply getting on the unicycle with the assistance of a wall or other support. With the continued assistance of that support, you mount the unicycle and try to pedal forward a little then back a little, until you feel comfortable enough to try and ride away from the wall. You continue this process until you can ride.

If after trying the "Crash Course" method, you feel the "wall" method is the more appropriate method of learning for you, then by all means proceed with the "wall" method.

"It is hard to fail, but it is worse never to have tried to succeed."

- *Theodore Roosevelt*

Chapter Twenty One
<u>BENEFITS OF UNICYCLING</u>

Unicycling has many benefits, some more apparent than others. As you learn to ride, and continue to ride over the years, you will experience some of those benefits and quite possibly new ones as well. This will depend on how proficient you become at riding.

Unicycling is excellent exercise and a great way to commute short distances. It's not uncommon to see a college student scooting around campus on a unicycle.

Unicycling is a great confidence booster, not only for children, but also for teens and adults. After all, learning to ride a unicycle proves that you can do <u>anything</u> if you are motivated and you practice.

Scientific research in Japan demonstrated that unicyclists improve their ability to concentrate, balance, and that their motor coordination is also sharpened.

73

These activities play an important role in the physical and mental development of the person. As a result, you will develop balance and agility unequalled by most people.

As you progress through the learning process, your built-in gyroscope, your brain, and your body will get "tuned" into each other like never before. You'll be amazed at the positive impact this will have over all other physical activities, not just now but for the rest of your natural life.

Recognizing this, the Japanese Educational Department officially integrated unicycle riding into their elementary school programs. Today, there are over a million unicyclists in Japan. GO JAPAN!

Chapter Twenty Two
UNICYCLING WEB LINKS

- **Ride The Unicycle Website**
  www.ridetheunicycle.com

- **Unicycling.Org Homepage**
  www.unicycling.org

- **The International Unicycling Federation**
  www.unicycling.org/iuf

- **The Unicycling Society of America**
  www.unicycling.org/usa/index.html

- **Unicycle.Com**
  www.unicycle.com

- **Unicyclist Community**
  www.unicyclist.com

"If you want to be successful, it's just this simple. Know what you are doing. Love what you are doing. And believe in what you are doing."

-Will Rogers

Chapter Twenty Three
ABOUT THE AUTHOR

Unicycling has been a part of my life since my 10th birthday when I received my first unicycle. It was an old Columbia 20" unicycle that my brother stripped, repainted, and cleaned up real nice. It's the same unicycle I ride today, although it's been modified a dozen times over the last 30+ years. I would venture to say that the unicycle is between 40 and 50 years old.

One of my fondest memories growing up was having three brothers who also enjoyed unicycle riding. We were the talk of the town because, back then, the only ones who rode the unicycle were clowns in the circus or something like that.

It didn't take long for all four of us to become expert unicyclists. We lived on our unicycles. Any game played on foot, we adapted to playing on the unicycle.

You name the game: basketball, baseball, football, hockey, tag, dodge-ball, BMX, Frisbee, racing, slalom, jump rope and even boxing. We played them all on unicycle.

Another one of my fondest unicycle memories was when I was 18. The Unicycling Society of America held a Unicycling rally during the city of Paterson's Great Falls Festival in Hinchcliff Stadium. The rally, one of the first of its kind in the area, had approximately 20 different competitive events. By the time the incredible day was over I had trophies in 17 of them and was interviewed by local news and media.

As my brothers got older, their passion for unicycling dwindled. My passion, however, continued to grow and is stronger today than ever. Over the years, I've designed and built many different unicycles of all sizes and shapes.

Unicycling has been very good to me and had I never learned my life would have been much different. The stories I have gathered over the last 30+ years could fill volumes.

As of this writing I'm 43 years old and have four boys of my own, two of which (Daniel who is 11 and Brian who is 9) are already riding the unicycle.

Unicycling is one of the legacies that I'll be leaving my family, hopefully, for generations to come. I get excited when I think ahead to a time when I'll be riding with my boys and possibly their children in a local parade or promotional event.

One of my aspirations is to someday ride across this great country of ours either by myself or with my boys, promoting the sport of unicycling.

Unicycling has been instrumental in making my life something special. I can only hope it does the same for you.

YOU CAN DO IT!

"Some men have thousands of reasons why they cannot do what they want to, when all they need is one reason why they can."

- Mary Frances Berry

Chapter Twenty Four
UNICYCLING SUPPORT

To facilitate continued support as you learn to ride the unicycle, I have provided a forum on my website, www.RideTheUnicycle.Com. The forum will make it easier for you to connect with me or other unicycling enthusiasts regarding different aspects of unicycling and learning to ride. Use and enjoy the forum; it was implemented for you and your continued success as you learn to ride.

In addition to my forum, I highly recommend the Unicyclist Community web forum found at www.unicyclist.com to learn more about what's happening in the unicycling community around the world. I highly recommend this web forum for the abundant amount of unicycling information. However, because this is an open forum, the topics and viewpoints sometimes deviate from the subject of unicycling. As a warning, some content may be inappropriate for children.

Happy Unicycling!
www.RideTheUnicycle.Com

www.RideTheUnicycle.Com

Quick Order Form

To receive additional copies of:

Ride The Unicycle ~ A Crash Course!

Please send this form along with your check or money order for the amount of $14.99 (plus $2.00 for postage in the U.S. or $3.00 International) to:

**Ride The Unicycle
202 Terrace Avenue
North Haledon NJ 07508-2620
United States of America**

Name: _____

Address: _____

City: _____ State: _____ Zip: _____

Country: _____

Email: _____

Or order on the World Wide Web at:

www.RideTheUnicycle.Com